Introduction

2 Timothy In-Depth Bible Study
Fight the good fight

Thank you so much for reading this book. I understand that there are other study guides available, so I really do appreciate you taking the time to read mine. As for this book, I give all the glory to God. Without Him, this wouldn't be possible.

You may notice that some passages were skipped, this is because I did not feel it on my heart to touch base on them. Therefore, there will be some gaps.

Throughout this study, when I refer to the enemy, I always use a lowercase letter, even if it's the first word in the sentence. I know that it may sound odd, considering we are taught not to do this, but this was intentional. So often we give the enemy power in our lives. Through anxiety, fear, depression, or whatever else it is that you are going through. I wanted to show you that he has no hold on a child of God. So when you see these "grammar issues", know that they were done on purpose. Use them as a reminder that satan has no hold on you. In the name of Jesus, you don't belong to him. You are God's, and God's alone.

2 Timothy 1:3-7

I love how much Paul cares for others. Not just for Timothy, but for all. I get a sense throughout his letters, that he has a genuine faith, and that he also cares deeply for others, and for their walk with Christ. I sense that he is not self-centered, but God centered. He says here that he serves God with a pure conscience. He does and says what he feels Christ would want him to, regardless of his own wants and needs.

Paul and his companions traveled throughout the region of Phrygia and Galatia, having been kept by the Holy Spirit from preaching the word in the province of Asia.

Acts 16:6

God, whom I serve in my spirit in preaching the gospel of his Son, is my witness how constantly I remember you in my prayers at all times; and I pray that now at last by God's will the way may be opened for me to come to you.

I long to see you so that I may impart to you some spiritual gift to make you strong— that is, that you and I may be mutually encouraged by each other's faith.

Romans 1:9-12

Paul doesn't just serve God, but He waits for God. Paul listens to God. If God says no, it's no, and if God says wait, he waits. So Paul serves God with a pure conscience, because he is trying his best to please God.

We also see Paul being an encouragement to others. This passage is a perfect example of that. Paul is sharing a tender moment with his son Timothy. He is remembering the genuine faith that was in Timothy's Mother and Grandmother. And not only is he remembering their genuine faith, but he is also encouraging Timothy, as well as reminding him, that the same genuine faith that he saw in them, he sees in him as well. Paul is also reminding Timothy to stir up the gift of God that is in him. Paul is telling Timothy not to be afraid, because God didn't give us the spirit of fear. God gave him everything that he needed to press on with the gift that God has entrusted him with.

This goes for you as well. I encourage you, and I urge you, do not neglect the gift that God has given you. There is a saying that I love and it's this. God does not call the equipped, He equips the called. Let's take a look at Moses. Moses was afraid of doing what God was asking of him, but God kept trying to remind Moses, that his strength didn't matter, his speech didn't matter, none of it mattered, because God was with him.

But Moses said to God, "Who am I that I should go to Pharaoh, and that I should bring the children of Israel out of Egypt?"

So He said, "I will certainly be with you.

Exodus 3:11-12

Moses was so afraid to step out and do what God was calling him to do. Moses had signs from God, Moses had assurance from God, yet, he was still afraid. But, if you notice, God never gave up on Moses. Moses said to send someone else, but God was basically saying, no, I want you. In the end, God even allowed Moses brother Aaron to go with him. God could have sent someone else, but Moses was the man for the job. You my friend, are the one for the job. Whatever God is asking you to do, He wants you for the job. You were made with a purpose. There is a specific job that God wants you to do. So you must decide. Will you be like Moses? Will you say no after no? Will you right here and right now, come to the conclusion that whatever God is asking you to do, you will do it? The fact is, I can talk to you until I am blue in the face, but the choice is ultimately up to you. No one can force you to listen to God. But God wants you to because God wants to give you the best life, and He can't do that if you don't listen to Him. If you go your own way, and don't follow His path, then that's never God's best for you. You have to remember that God loves you. God's plans are never to harm you or hurt you, but to prosper you. That doesn't mean that the journey will be easy. Sometimes, the journey getting there is the hardest part. I look at it like a bridge. The bridge is your faith. You can choose to walk over this bridge of faith, not knowing what's on the other side, or you can be too afraid to go over it. But remember this, if you never go over it, then you will never get to see the beautiful plans that await you on the other side. I truly hope and pray, that you make the right choice.

2 Timothy 1:7

God did not create us to fear, instead, He created us to conqueror. This is why through Him, we are more than conquerors.

Yet in all these things we are more than conquerors through Him who loved us.

Romans 8:37

This verse holds dear to me, because I suffered for a really long time with crippling anxiety. To tell you the truth, I still fight it to this day. Take it from someone who allowed fear to grip her for so long, God never intended for us to be afraid. We do have the power inside of us to conquer fear, and I know this from experience. As I said, I still fight it, but I am so much farther than where I was when this all started about 3 years ago. I say this for anyone else who has been dealing with fear, YOU CAN CONQUER IT! Unfortunately, there is no overnight cure, and it takes a lot of hard work, I can attest to that, but you can do it. Do you know what drives that fear away?

God's love.

perfect love casts out fear

1 John 4:18

God's power

Behold, I give you the authority to trample on serpents and scorpions, and over all the power of the enemy, and nothing shall by any means hurt you.

Luke 10:19

You are of God, little children, and have overcome them, because He who is in you is greater than he who is in the world.

1 John 4:4

God's strength, God's comfort, God's protection, God's patience, God, God, and God again. The fear that I endured, brought me to a place with God, that I don't know if I would have achieved, if not for that fear. So although the fear was so crippling, God worked all things together for my good, and brought me closer to Him. God showed me that He will take care of me, that He will comfort me, that I can rely on Him, that He cares how I feel, that He will protect me, love me, and so much more. God doesn't want His children to be afraid. God did not give us the spirit of fear, but instead of love, power, and a sound mind. You have to come to terms with the fact that God will never leave you nor forsake you. You have to realize that God was protecting you long before you were even born. When He died on the cross, He was protecting us from ourselves, from death, from the enemy, from separation, etc. He was showing us His great love for us. God has already proven that He will always take care of you, so stop doubting Him. He has you exactly where you are meant to be, in the palm of His hands.

Have you ever told yourself that you don't know how much longer you can hold on? I have learned that it's OK to let go. Why? Because I came to find out, that when I let go, when I fully surrendered, God was still holding me up, because I was never truly the one holding onto anything in the first place. It was God holding onto me all along. It just took a long time for me to see it. I was trying to control everything around me, because everything made me afraid. Whether it was walking into the kitchen, or outside the door, I was scared. So what did I do? I tried to control. Control my circumstances, control my surroundings, etc. I came to realize, that I was never truly the one in control in the first place, God was. In this journey with Him, I have come to know Him for being the loving, faithful God that He is. I have seen His character, and I have seen His grace. I have seen His mercy, and I have seen His patience. I have come to know Him, and once you come to know Him on a much deeper level than a surface knowledge, things become so much clearer. Through spending time with Him, reading His word, praying, etc, I have learned how indescribable He truly is. I have known Him for as long as I can remember, but never like this. So fear can be crippling, tiresome, and sorrowful, but I have come to learn that God will show you why you shouldn't fear, if you let Him. You will come to realize that the answer is always, because God.

If God is for us, who can be against us?

Romans 8:31

The LORD is my light and my salvation;
Whom shall I fear?
The LORD is the strength of my life;
Of whom shall I be afraid?
When the wicked came against me
To eat up my flesh,
My enemies and foes,
They stumbled and fell.
Though an army may encamp against me,
My heart shall not fear;
Though war may rise against me,
In this I will be confident.

One thing I have desired of the LORD,
That will I seek:
That I may dwell in the house of the LORD
All the days of my life,
To behold the beauty of the LORD,
And to inquire in His temple.
For in the time of trouble
He shall hide me in His pavilion;
In the secret place of His tabernacle
He shall hide me;
He shall set me high upon a rock.

Psalm 27:1-5

Another passage that is great when you feel afraid, which is one of my favorites, is Psalm 91. If you ever feel fearful, or anxious, I suggest you read it. It helps me, and I hope it helps you as well.

If you are trying to fight fear, keep fighting. Don't give up. Even if it feels like it's taking a really long time, don't stop fighting. Remember, you are not fighting alone.

The LORD will fight for you; you need only to be still.

Exodus 14:14

Let us not become weary in doing good, for at the proper time we will reap a harvest if we do not give up.

Galatians 6:9

If you are in the midst of a battle with anxiety, I wrote a book with my journal entries that may help you. It's called, "Breaking Chains: The diary of a Christian woman who overcame anxiety".

I pray for anyone who is reading this, if you are dealing with fear, that you feel a sense of peace. That you keep fighting and remember to keep your eyes on God, He will guide you through. Trust Him.

2 Timothy 1:8-12

If I jumped in front of a bullet just to save your life, would you be ashamed of me? If you owed a debt that you couldn't afford, and I graciously paid it for you, would you again, be ashamed of me? Jesus paid a debt that we could not afford. He came down, leaving behind His kingdom, to become a man, just to save us. He had so much, yet left it all behind, for love. He left it all behind, because He loves you. Jesus came to earth, and He suffered. He suffered and then He died, to save you. To pay a debt that you and I couldn't afford. I will never be ashamed of that kind of love. You could mock me, persecute me, or kill me, but my heart will always remain steadfast for my God.

Sometimes people won't accept what you share. I had an encounter with a woman once, and I came home a bit confused. I couldn't understand why I was showing someone the greatest gift that they could ever get, but refused it. I just didn't understand. But then God showed me this.

The god of this age has blinded the minds of unbelievers, so that they cannot see the light of the gospel that displays the glory of Christ, who is the image of God.

2 Corinthians 4:4

This scripture made me understand that they were not accepting this gift, because satan had blinded them from seeing the truth. But, this doesn't mean that we just simply stop spreading the good news, no, just the opposite. It means that we keep fighting and keep spreading the gospel, regardless of what others think of us. I love this scripture in 2 Corinthians.

If we are "out of our mind," as some say, it is for God; if we are in our right mind, it is for you. For Christ's love compels us, because we are convinced that one died for all, and therefore all died. And he died for all, that those who live should no longer live for themselves but for him who died for them and was raised again.

2 Corinthians 5:13-15

Some people will look at us like we are crazy, and that's OK. That person that you talk to today who thinks you're nuts, could be that person in a year from now who accepts Jesus, all because you planted the seed, someone watered it, and through the power of the Holy Spirit, it grew. You may never know what happens to that seed once you plant it. That seed could flourish into a pastor, a speaker, a Godly Mom, a Godly wife, a Godly sister, a Godly friend, etc. Maybe that seed will grown into someone who saves one, or many others. You should never be afraid or ashamed of your faith. As I said before, you wouldn't be ashamed of someone who saved your life, and paid off your debt. You would be so thankful that you would tell everyone what they did for you.

If we suffer for the gospel, then let us do it together, as one. We were saved. Not because we deserved it, and not because we did so many good things to receive it, but we were saved because we are loved by a beautiful God. You share Jesus, because you love Jesus, it's that simple. Yes, we may suffer as we do, we may get someone who looks at us like we're crazy, and we may even get huffed at, but that's OK. Because guess what? They are not the one that you have to face in the end, God is. I know the God who I believe in, and I know that He is real. I have felt His love, His guidance, His presence, His patience, His compassion, mercy, grace, and so much more. He is undeniably real. So I am not ashamed, because like Paul, I know whom I have believed, and I also know that when the time comes when I see Jesus face to face, when I am standing in front of Him, in all of His glory, I will be glad that I tried my best. I believe a lot of people, when they get to see Jesus face to face, they will wish that they would have been braver, bolder, more courageous, and more willing to be used by Him. Don't let that be you. Don't let your fear or your feelings keep you from being used by God. Because one day, you will come face to face with Jesus, and wish that you didn't let fear, feelings, circumstances, or your situation get in the way of what God was calling you to do. I pray that those of you who needed to hear this, don't just let this be a moment where you say that sounds good, but I pray that it's a moment that changes you into becoming the person that God intended for you to be. Don't just read these words thinking that they sound good, but let them change you. Let them put fire in your bones to do something more. To be who God is calling you to be. I pray that God sinks this deep into your soul, that you take it to heart, and really think on it as you lay your head down tonight. God has a plan for you, don't let anything stop you from it.

Remember, the only one that can stop you from doing God's will, is you.

2 Timothy 1:15-18

Here we see that Paul was deserted by those in Asia. He even went as far as to name two of them. It seems that there was one person, who was not ashamed of his chains. Onesiphorus helped Paul, and he even went as far as to search him out. Here, Paul is blessing him and his household. This is a perfect example of how one person can make all the difference in someone's life. Will you be that one person? The one who cares about someone's needs before your own? Will you be that one person, who drops what they are doing, to seek out the lost or the ones in need? Will you be that one person, willing to be used by God? Will that person, be you?

2 Timothy 2:3-4

Throughout the bible, we see clearly that we will endure hardship. This passage reminds us, that we are soldiers of Jesus Christ. Whether you are a good one or not, is up to you. Being a good soldier of Jesus Christ, means many things. One of them is this. We do not entangle ourselves with the worries of this life. If you are in a war, and enemies are pursuing you with arrows in hand, what would you do? If you stay in the fight, then that's honorable, but, if you run away, and desert your brothers and sisters fighting this war with you, then what? If you leave the battlefield, because you are worried of something else of this world, then the enemy will still chase you, but now you have the opportunity to be blindsided. You see, if you take your eyes off of the battle sitting right in front of you, you are now left with no sword in hand. You have now left your armor and your fight behind, to instead of sword, hold the things of this world. Let me clarify a bit. God has shown me that He wants me to keep writing books. I can choose to keep doing as He asks, even when it's hard, or I can quit. I can decide that it takes too much time, and I can just quit. If I do this, I am walking away from what God is calling me to do at this moment in my life. If I walk away from it, it doesn't mean that the enemy will stop chasing after my demise, it only means that I am now being disobedient to God. But, I am choosing to be a good soldier of Jesus Christ, I am choosing to see where these books lead, and I am choosing to follow Christ, no matter the cost. Eventually, I will see where they lead, but for now, I am choosing to trust. Trust that God has a plan, and trust that even if it's hard, even if it takes time, and even if it takes up a lot of my time, I will keep pushing, and I will see what God has planned for me. I am choosing to draw my sword, keep my armor on, and fight. Because I am choosing to please the one who enlisted me, my Lord and Savior, Jesus Christ.

2 Timothy 2:5

When we fight, we fight according to the rules. There are no shortcuts in God's path. God has specific things in mind for you. You can't go around this or that, because it's uncomfortable or hard. You have to be willing to be uncomfortable at times. Not everything is going to be easy. Just because you know God's path, doesn't mean that it's smooth sailing, although sometimes it may be. In my experience, most of the time, when God calls you to do something, there is a laying down of self that occurs. Sometimes the path that you were originally on, was so far to the left, that now you have to go through some things, just to get to the real path on the right. And to do that, is hard. I can attest that it can be extremely difficult at times. Sometimes you want to give up and quit, and sometimes you feel so fired up that you want to keep going. This life is like running a marathon. It can be hard and it's not easy sometimes. Your legs get weary and you sometimes have to crawl your way to the finish line. And the times when you just can't go on anymore, God carries you. He carries you in His loving arms, and He gives you the strength that you need to keep going. God never gives up on you, so never give up on Him. He knows exactly what He is doing, and He will do it. All you have to do, is trust Him.

The one who calls you is faithful, and he will do it.

1 Thessalonians 5:24

2 Timothy 2:5

Keep working hard, and don't give up. A farmer plows, plants, and waits for his seeds to grow. His hard work brings forth a harvest that he first partakes in. You too, after you have plowed, planted, and waited, will reap a harvest. But don't forget the last one I mentioned, time. It takes time. Sometimes weeks, sometimes months, and sometimes years. I am currently coming up on my fourth year of waiting, and I can attest to how hard it is. It's so difficult at times. Filled with tears, hope, persistence, sorrow, and everything in between. But, I am still fighting. I know that one day, I will see the harvest. I know that one day, I will see where God has been leading me. Sometimes, I write in tears. As I am writing this for you at this moment, I am also in tears. But if I have to write in tears, to get to where God wants me, then so be it. I refuse to give up, and I really hope that you have been encouraged to do the same. I know waiting is hard, but please, don't stop fighting. God knows exactly what He is doing. You need to focus on planting the seeds, and trust God to send the rain.

2 Timothy 2:7

May the Lord give you understanding in all things.

2 Timothy 2:8-12

Here we see that Paul is fighting. He is not only fighting for Jesus, but for us. For everyone of God's people. He is also fighting for those who don't believe, so that they may have salvation as well. So although Paul suffers, even to the point of being in chains, he endures it. He endures it for that which is not chained, the word of God, and he counts the rest as loss.

Yet indeed I also count all things loss for the excellence of the knowledge of Christ Jesus my Lord, for whom I have suffered the loss of all things, and count them as rubbish, that I may gain Christ

Philippians 3:8

What Jesus said, says it all.

Then He said to them all, "If anyone desires to come after Me, let him deny himself, and take up his cross daily, and follow Me. For whoever desires to save his life will lose it, but whoever loses his life for My sake will save it.

Luke 9:23-24

Here Paul is acknowledging that he is taking up his cross, and following after Jesus. We died with Jesus, we shall live with Jesus, we endure, and we will also reign. We endure the hardships that come with taking up our cross and following Jesus, but, the day will come, when we will reign with Him. All of the fight, all of the hardship, all of the tears, and all of the enduring, will lead to a place that was worth the fight in this life. I have felt God's presence, His peace, and His love. If I have to fight for however long God has placed me on this earth, so that one day I can be with Him in heaven, then I fight. While on earth, we see mere glimpses of Him. I could never fathom, I could never imagine, what it will be like to be in His presence 24/7. I understand that His presence is with us now, but you know what I mean when I say these words. I believe that anything I could ever imagine, is nothing compared to what it will really be like. Jesus is worth the fight.

So when the mountain stands in your way, tell it to move. If it doesn't move, go over it. Because for me, I'm either going over this mountain, or I'm going through it. I'm not stopping, and I won't quit.

2 Timothy 2:13

God is so faithful. Even when we stray, even when we falter, and even when we are not faithful to Him, He always remains faithful to us. He is such a good God. I have seen His faithfulness so many times over. Whether it's when I feel like I can't go on anymore, or whether I feel like I have no fight left, I have seen Him comfort me, and give me the strength that I needed to keep going. I have seen Him care about things that matter to me, even when they may be so small to others, and I have seen Him show me love, even when I am upset. I don't serve Him because I get something in return. No, I serve Him because I love Him. I serve Him because He is such a wonderful God, and I wouldn't want to follow anyone or anything else. He was there in my beginning, and He will be there in my end. He is faithful, and He remains faithful.

2 Timothy 2:14-19

Remind people of these things. Urge people before the Lord, not to go after words that have no benefit to others, or themselves. Do not be ashamed of the Gospel, and do everything as if it's being done for the Lord.

And whatever you do, do it heartily, as to the Lord and not to men, knowing that from the Lord you will receive the reward of the inheritance; for you serve the Lord Christ.

Colossians 3:23-24

Do the things that please God, not man. Work hard to understand the truth.

If you allow things of this world to sink into your mind, they will spread like a cancer. One leads to the next, which leads to the next, until it consumes you. Be on your guard and fight the good fight. Deny the things of this world, whether in word or thought. These things are useless and do nothing for your walk with Christ. Useless babbling and profanity, what good could they possibly do for you?

Do you not know that a little leaven leavens the whole lump?

1 Corinthians 5:6

Do not buy into those who say that the resurrection has past. They do nothing but lead others away from the path.

Either way, regardless of what others may say, the solid foundation of our God, still stands. God knows those who are His.

2 Timothy 2:20-26

There are two types of people. One for honor, and one for dishonor. If you once were for dishonor, and you cleansed yourself from such, if you are now a follower of Christ, you are now God's vessel, for honor. You are now holy and set apart for His good works. We are but the vessel. God is the potter, and we are the clay. You can allow Him to shape and mold you into a vessel used for His glory, or you can decide that you want to go your own way, and mold yourself. But remember, just as a mug can not mold itself, neither can you. Not well anyway. The potters hands are needed to remove the impurities, and to clean up the things that don't belong. Only God knows the deep things that need to be removed. Even we ourselves do not see it in it's entirety, what needs to be removed. Only God sees exactly what needs to stay and grow, and what needs to be cut off. Just as one who sees in a mirror, sees things backwards, God sees them clearly. The mirror is foggy for us, but God sees it in it's entirety. Only God can prepare us for the good works that He has chosen for us. So we flee from the things of this world, and entrust ourselves to our Father. We flee from the things of this world, and pursue the things of God instead. We avoid foolish disputes and arguments, as they are no benefit to anyone, and only produce turmoil. Arguing makes people bitter and resentful. There is no honor in quarreling with others, for the sake of quarreling. Perhaps someone is quarreling because they are trying to find the truth, this is not foolish. This is someone who is genuinely trying to find the truth. But it becomes foolish when someone is quarreling with you, only to generate strife, or as some would say, trying to push your buttons. Therefore, we must not quarrel with anyone, but be gentle to all, because this is the will of our Father. To love all, to teach with patience, and to be humble enough to correct those who oppose us, gently. If you do this harshly, would this make the quarreler want to come to Christ? I say no, but, if you were to be gentle, even when they are irate, even when they are mean, or even when they disagree, this may lead them to the truth, and in turn, save their soul. It is God who works in and through you, and it is God who changes the hearts and minds of those who hear. Our job is to speak the words that we are given, and to entrust the Holy Spirit to do the changing of hearts. We can only hope and pray that they may come to the truth, come to their senses, and escape the snare of the devil.

This is a separate note for those of you who are waiting for the prodigal to return. Don't give up hope. If you have been praying for your son, your daughter, your friend, your family member, or anyone else to come to the Lord, don't stop praying. Keep having faith and hope that God will change their hearts and minds, and let them see the truth. I pray over whoever is reading this, I pray that God will give you the strength to keep going, keep praying, and keep praising in the waiting. I pray that you don't give up hope, but keep your hope in our wonderful Father who never fails. Even if it's taking what seems like forever, don't, stop, praying. Prayer changes people, and situations. Be patient, be hopeful, and trust in the Lord.

Be joyful in hope, patient in affliction, faithful in prayer.

Romans 12:12

2 Timothy 3:1-9

We have seen over the course of time, that people have become more about themselves. They have become more about their wants and needs, rather than what God wants. We have seen people straying from the truth, become impatient, caring only for themselves, etc. We have seen the world change for the worse. People are losing their zeal and fervency for the Lord, people are changing, some becoming proud, blaspheming God, disobedient to parents, etc. People are looking for the benefit of themselves, rather than the benefit of others. Turn from these people! There are some who claim to be your friends, yet they try to turn you from the truth at every chance. They come into households, and feed lies to gullible people. They are learning, but none of it is the truth.

These people may have a form of godliness, but they deny it's power. These people resist the truth, but their foolishness will become know to all.

2 Timothy 3:10-11

Paul endured many things for the sake of the gospel. Just as Timothy carefully followed in these footsteps, we should do as well. And just as God delivered Paul out of His many trials, He will deliver you too. Sometimes we get caught up in how long we have been waiting for something, and we forget to remember that He is God, and we are not. God's timing is perfect, and if He has not answered your prayer just yet, He has a reason. Sometimes we are not meant to understand everything, but to trust the One who does.

Trust in the LORD with all your heart,
And lean not on your own understanding;

Proverbs 3:5

We trust God, and we don't lean on what our understanding of the situation is. We trust God to make our paths straight, and we submit to His will, no matter the cost.

In all your ways acknowledge Him,
And He shall direct your paths.

Proverbs 3:6

2 Timothy 3:12

All who desire to live a life for Christ, will face many trials, and we will suffer persecution. Maybe you are someone battling your parents who want you in a different religion, or none at all. Maybe you have been ridiculed for your faith. I urge you to take a stand, and do not desert your faith. Keep your fervency for the Lord, and do not falter. Remain steadfast.

But whosoever shall deny me before men, him will I also deny before my Father which is in heaven.

Matthew 10:33

2 Timothy 3:13-15

As time goes on, evil will grow all the more. Impostors, false prophets, and those seeking your ruin will grow all the more. These people will deceive and be deceived. But, you must hold fast to what you have learned. Hold the truth in your hearts, and bind them around you. Keep continuing in the things which you have learned, letting no one lead you away from what you have known to be true. Do not be gullible with their cunning and deceitful words. Just as Eve believed the deceitful words of a serpent, we must also remember that we too can be deceived, therefore we must stand guard. We must keep watch. Hold onto what you know to be true, and let no one turn you from the truth. Keep your faith in Jesus Christ, for which you have salvation through His name, through your faith in Him.

2 Timothy 3:16-17

Some people may say that the bible was written by people, not God, so this discredits the fact that it's from

God. This scripture clearly shows you that God spoke through these people, to write the truth of God. Paul says that ALL scripture is given by inspiration of God. The meaning of inspiration, is the process of being mentally stimulated to do or feel something. If the Holy Spirit speaks through you, and you are holding the pen, it is still from God, even if you were inspired to write about how God has worked in your life. God still put it on your heart to do so, and you are but a vessel.

Also, if you notice, the accounts of these peoples lives, they not only uplift us, but strengthen us. Even in Psalms, we see cries for help, and then deliverance. Look at the character of God throughout the bible. Numerous accounts, by numerous people. Scripture truly does equip you for every good work. If you read the bible, you will notice that God's character is consistent. He truly never changes.

For I am the LORD, I do not change

Malachi 3:6

Jesus Christ is the same yesterday, today, and forever.

Hebrews 13:8

When you see the consistency of our God, you see that He is good, He is faithful, He is loving, He is protective of His people, etc. These words in the bible are good for teaching, for correction, etc, because they are good words. His character is what we all know to be right. What we are taught in His word, are what we know to be morally correct. So keep these words with you, and never let them go.

2 Timothy 4:1-8

The day will come when Jesus returns. For some this will be a glorious day, and for others, a dreadful one.

We will give an account, and we will face God, knowing in our hearts if we tried our best, or faltered. For now, always be ready. Preach the word of God, share the good news of Jesus Christ, and don't stop. Be ready, no matter what season you are in. If you are in a waiting season, be ready, a sorrowful season, be ready, etc. Convince, rebuke, exhort, and endure anything that comes along with it. As a fellow servant of the Lord used to say, obey God, and leave the consequences to Him.

Some people refuse to hear sound doctrine. They want to live their own way, so they seek people who teach what it is that they want to hear. Be careful and watchful in all things. Endure the trials that you face, and keep doing God's work. Just as Paul was prepared to be used as a drink offering, you too be willing and ready.

Paul fought the good fight, finished his race, and kept the faith, regardless of his surroundings, regardless of his circumstances, and regardless of what anyone said. He worked towards the unseen. He suffered knowing that there was something greater waiting for him. He suffered and fought with faith. The faith that is in and through Jesus Christ. You too, abide in Christ, as He abides in you.

Abide in Me, and I in you. As the branch cannot bear fruit of itself, unless it abides in the vine, neither can you, unless you abide in Me.

John 15:4

Jesus answered and said to him, "If anyone loves Me, he will keep My word; and My Father will love him, and We will come to him and make Our home with him.

John 14:23

We may struggle here on earth, but we struggle with the hope and faith, that one day we will be with our Savior Jesus Christ. One day, this suffering will be worth it. So we look forward to not the seen, but the unseen. We look forward to what lies ahead, throwing off what lies behind, and we run our race. I urge you here and now, take this same stand with me. Fight the good fight, and finish the race that you have in God through Christ Jesus. Keep your faith, and Fight.

2 Timothy 4:16-18

Even though with human eyes, it may have looked like Paul was alone in his fight, he was never truly alone. At his first defense, all forsook him, but Paul knew that he was not standing alone. Remember, whatever fight you are in, whatever battle you are facing, you are not in it alone. As we know, God does not change. Therefore, He fought for His people then, and He still fights for His people now. He delivered His people then, and He still delivers them now. He healed His people then, and He still heals His people now. Don't forget who our God is. He can do abundantly more than you could ever ask, think, or imagine. Whatever you feel in this moment, whatever it is that you are fighting for, give it to God. Trust God to fight for you, and with you. You have to realize that you are NEVER alone. Whatever you walk through, whether valley, mountain, or the depths of the sea, you have a beautiful, wonderful, and loving God, walking through them with you. If it feels dark, God will be your guiding light. Don't lose your focus, and don't lose your fight. God will fight for you, so trust Him. Be still, and trust Him. Keep running your race, and keep fighting the good fight. Because on that beautiful day, when you see Jesus face to face, you will be glad you did.

The Lord Jesus Christ be with your spirit. Grace be with you. Amen.

To view more books by Tentmaker Ministries, please visit
Tm-Ministries.com

www.ingramcontent.com/pod-product-compliance
Lightning Source LLC
Chambersburg PA
CBHW011219120626
46545CB00008B/3060